— THE **UNTOLD STORY** OF —

ANNIE TURNBO MALONE

HAIR CARE MILLIONAIRE

BY DR. ARTIKA R. TYNER

Consultant:
Dr. De Anna Reese
Professor
California State University, Fresno

CAPSTONE PRESS
a capstone imprint

Published by Capstone Press, an imprint of Capstone
1710 Roe Crest Drive, North Mankato, Minnesota 56003
capstonepub.com

Library of Congress Cataloging-in-Publication Data is available on
the Library of Congress website.

ISBN: 9781669004967 (hardcover)
ISBN: 9781669004912 (paperback)
ISBN: 9781669004929 (ebook PDF)

Summary: Most people know about Madam C.J. Walker's success selling hair
care products for Black women in the early 1900s. Before she started her own
business, though, she worked for Annie Turnbo Malone. Malone built a huge
business creating hair care and cosmetic products for Black women. Uncover
Malone's story and how it connects to Walker's story.

Editorial Credits
Editor: Ericka Smith; Designer: Sarah Bennett; Media Researcher: Svetlana
Zhurkin; Production Specialist: Katy LaVigne

Image Credits
Alamy: IanDagnall Computing, 21; Associated Press: The Compound
Foundation/Amy Sussman, 29; Collection of the Smithsonian National Museum
of African American History and Culture: 4, 15, 22, 23; Getty Images: Bettmann,
8, Buyenlarge, 27; Library of Congress: Prints and Photographs Division, 17,
Prints and Photographs Division/Carol M. Highsmith, 6; The New York Public
Library: Schomburg Center for Research in Black Culture, 7, 13; Shutterstock:
Everett Collection, 19, 20, Julia Khimich (background), cover (right) and
throughout, Nadegda Rozova (background), cover (left) and throughout, Tainar,
9; The State Historical Society of Missouri: Black History Photograph Collection,
S0336.21, cover, 25; U.S. Patent and Trademark Office: 11

TABLE OF CONTENTS

Words in **bold** are in the glossary.

A YOUNG INVENTOR

Annie Turnbo Malone had enjoyed chemistry since she was a young girl. She was naturally curious and loved to experiment. She read every chemistry and biology book that she could find.

Malone wanted to create a solution to a challenge facing Black women. Many Black women in the late 1800s and early 1900s used heat and chemicals to straighten their hair. But this resulted in breakage and hair loss. Malone wanted to help Black women grow healthy and strong hair.

Malone experimented with different combinations of chemicals, herbs, mineral oils, and vegetables to create hair care products. Eventually, she created the right mix—her Wonderful Hair Grower—and started what would become a million-dollar business.

Most people have heard of Madam C.J. Walker, who became a famous Black businesswoman in the beauty industry. But Malone's story is not as well known. This is the story of her journey as a hair care pioneer.

FACT There are other Black women who were millionaires during Malone's time. In the mid-1800s, Mary Ellen Pleasant was a successful entrepreneur. She invested in the stock market and in real estate and used the profits to open laundries and boardinghouses in California.

A CURIOUS MIND

Malone was born in Metropolis, Illinois, in 1869. She was the tenth of eleven children. Her parents, Robert Turnbo and Isabella Cook, were born into slavery. After slavery ended, Malone's father became a farmer, and her family struggled to make ends meet. Her parents died when she was young, so she was raised by her sister in Peoria, Illinois.

A mural of Metropolis, Illinois

A Black woman with straightened hair in the late 1800s

As early as 14 years old, Malone was known for styling hair using the latest trends. At the time, Black women wanted long, straight hair—a **Eurocentric** standard of beauty. Wearing their hair straight sometimes earned Black women more privileges. Malone had an **inquisitive** mind, so she experimented with products and methods to straighten curly hair. She tried them on her sisters and friends.

Making a Living After the Abolition of Slavery

Malone was born just four years after slavery was abolished with the passage of the Thirteenth Amendment to the Constitution. Although Black people were no longer enslaved, many were left without jobs, education, and housing. Some stayed on the same farms where they had been enslaved and became **sharecroppers** or wage laborers. Others moved north hoping for better opportunities.

Workers on a peanut farm in the late 1890s

Malone also used herbs in her hair products. She learned to grow herbs from her aunt, who was an herbal doctor.

Malone's family wanted her to become a dressmaker like her older sister Ada. But Malone was passionate about helping Black women grow healthy hair and build their confidence. She knew she had a gift. She chose instead to work with her sister Laura Roberts to create new hair products.

Malone used geranium oil in some of her hair products.

CHAPTER 2

FROM VISION TO REALITY

Malone and Roberts worked tirelessly to create their first product. They wanted to address the challenge of dry, brittle hair that breaks easily. Malone and Roberts successfully created a shampoo that helped restore hair. They began demonstrating its positive effects and selling it to customers.

Soon they were selling their new products door-to-door. Since businesses were segregated, Black women were not able to shop in most of their local stores. Instead, the sisters visited their customers in their homes, which helped them create a personal connection. In 1900, Malone and Roberts rented a two-story house in Lovejoy, Illinois, to open their own store.

Black Women and the Hair Care Industry

Black women have been transforming the hair care industry for a long time. In 1898, Lyda Newman created and patented a hairbrush designed for Black women. She influenced the design of hairbrushes for generations to come. In 1917, Nobia Franklin founded the Franklin School of Beauty Culture. The school trained Black hairstylists who served the needs of the Houston community. Franklin also created a manufacturing plant to produce her hair care products.

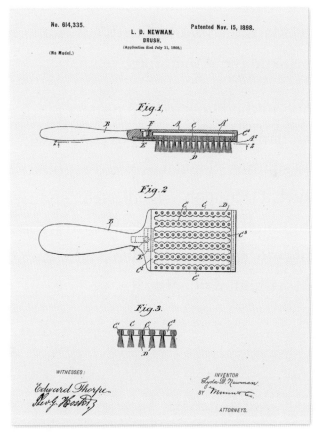

Drawings of Lyda Newman's hairbrush

Malone discovered a connection between poor **hygiene** and hair breakage and loss for Black women. Black women had limited access to clean living areas. Many lived in poor communities that did not have good **sanitation**. They couldn't wash their hair regularly. Many also worked with hazardous chemicals like bleach and lye at their jobs.

Malone studied how to help protect Black women's hair from damage. She started to experiment and came up with a solution. She developed a **regimen** of using a special herbal shampoo, a medicated conditioner, and a pressing comb, which used heat to straighten hair. Using this process, Black women could straighten their hair without damaging it.

SHAMPOO THE HAIR AND RINSE SEVERAL TIMES

PRESS and DRESS YOUR OWN HAIR

If you can COMB your hair, you can PRESS your hair with this wonderful Steel Comb Straightener. It imparts to the hair short or long, a new and brilliant lustre that you had never before. After you have washed or shampooed your hair and scalp, you can finish the job of DRYING, STRAIGTENING and DRESSING as nicely as any hairdresser with the use of the

MASTER COMB

You can keep your hair in the GOOD-TO-LOOK-AT condition for a lifetime, for less money than it would cost to visit a first-class hairdresser for four treatments. It requires no skill to use it... Simply use it like an ordinary comb, pushing it thru the hair in the direction the hair lays, turning its back downward on the portion that the teeth have passed thru—and you have performed at one stroke the operation that most hairdressers have paid $25 to learn to do.

KEEP YOUR DAUGHTERS HAIR

looking its best at all times with the MASTER COMB, and save the expense and trouble of taking them to the hairdressers. It works so easily and the job is done so quickly and stylishly that you enjoy giving them home treatments quite as much as they will enjoy receiving them. To each purchaser of the MASTER COMB a printed instruction of "Shampooing the Hair and How to Treat It" will be furnished FREE.

THE MASTER COMB $3.00 EACH
Foreign Countries $3.25

AGENTS AND DEALERS GET YOUR PROPOSITION

This is one of the rare occasions when you are able to connect up with real "Sell on Sight" articles. Something that every woman will buy on sight because it actually saves them $12 to $25 every year. Our Agents are coining money. Why not YOU? Write at once for terms and make your spare time earn large profits.

THE MASTER COMB & SPECIALTY COMPANY

Dept. C. B.   126 Liberty Street   New York, U. S. A.

MASTER JR.
$1.25
FOREIGN COUNTRIES
$1.50

AFTER HAIR IS WASHED RUB THE MASTER HAIR GROWER IN SCALP THOROUGHLY

HEAT MASTER COMB ONE TO THREE MINUTES ON OIL, ALCOHOL, GAS OR COAL STOVE

PASS TEETH THRU HAIR AND WITH SLIGHT TURN OF THE WRIST BRING HEAVY BACK DOWN ON PORTION TEETH HAVE PASSED THRU

AFTER PRESSED IN STYLE DESIRED, THE BEAUTY OF YOUR HAIR WILL BE WONDERFUL TO BEHOLD

Please Mention The Crusader

An advertisement from around 1920 for a pressing comb

As more customers tried their products, the sisters became well known in the Black community. People traveled to Illinois just to purchase their products. Malone taught them how to use the products properly.

In 1902, Malone moved the headquarters of her business to St. Louis, Missouri. She named her brand Poro. The word *Poro* comes from a West African culture. Malone used the word because she wanted to show that she was proud of her African roots.

In St. Louis, Malone continued to expand her business for nearly three decades. And she used her success to help uplift the Black community—both in St. Louis and across the country.

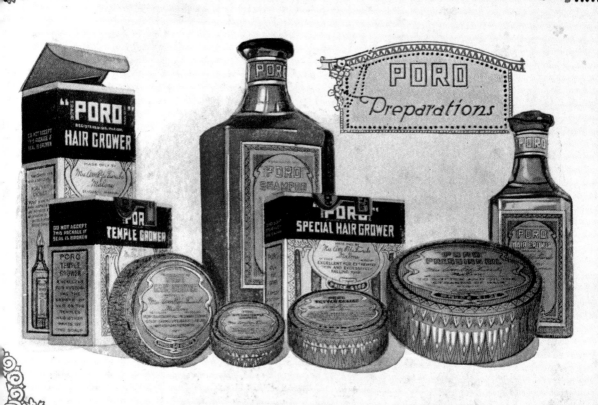

Poro products in the 1920s

BUILDING A BUSINESS EMPIRE

Malone's business grew rapidly after the 1904 St. Louis World's Fair. People from around the world visited the city during the fair. They bought new products from local sellers.

This was the opportunity Malone had been waiting for. Black women from near and far purchased her products. After these women used her products, they told friends and family how the products improved their hair. They could now grow long, silky, and healthy hair.

Soon Malone's products were used worldwide. With this new popularity, more women wanted to join the Poro team and sell its products.

The 1904 St. Louis World's Fair

Malone was determined to make the American Dream a reality for herself and other Black women. She decided to focus on creating wealth by providing jobs to Black people across the nation—especially Black women.

Malone's vision for her business was influenced by Dr. Booker T. Washington, an educator and founder of Tuskegee Institute in Alabama. Dr. Washington believed the future of the Black community depended on developing practical job skills. With job skills, they could help build a strong **economy** within the Black community. This would help them create wealth.

Dr. Booker T. Washington

A domestic worker in the 1920s

Poro became the sort of business that gave its employees a chance to create their own opportunities. Poro sales **agents**' lives changed as they built new careers and increased their earnings. Many were very successful. Poro agents earned at least 10 times more than women who worked as **domestics.**

One example is Sarah Breedlove Walker, better known as Madam C.J. Walker. Walker famously went from being a laundress to working as a Poro agent to creating her own products and becoming a millionaire.

Madam C.J. Walker

Madam C.J. Walker struggled with hair problems herself. She became a Poro agent around 1904. In 1905, she moved to Denver, Colorado, and continued to sell Poro products. Walker said she had a dream that revealed to her a new recipe for hair products. After she woke from the dream, she began developing new products. She started her own business in 1906 and created a grooming process she called the Walker System.

Walker sold her products throughout the South. She went on to build her business in Pittsburgh, Pennsylvania, and then Indianapolis, Indiana, where she built a factory, a salon, and a training center.

In 1916, Walker moved to New York. She switched her focus from daily business operations to the arts and social causes—including the National Association for the Advancement of Colored People's anti-lynching movement. After quickly becoming one of the wealthiest Black businesswomen in the world, Walker died in 1919 at the relatively young age of 51. But her family has worked hard to sustain her legacy—through books, a legacy center in her honor in Indianapolis, and even a new line of products named after her.

Poro College in St. Louis

In 1918, Malone built Poro College. It served as a training center for the Poro agents. It also housed Poro's business offices, manufacturing plants, and laboratories. And because Malone wanted Poro College to serve the Black community of St. Louis, it also included things such as an auditorium, a rooftop garden, and a bakery.

Poro College was an important source of education and job opportunities for Black women—and some Black men. Black people could not work in white salons. Their typical job options were working as domestics or sharecroppers—in poor conditions for low wages. Over Malone's career, she created jobs for 75,000 women ranging in age from 16 to 80.

Malone taught her agents about hair care before they started selling her products. At Poro, agents served as beauty **consultants** while selling Poro products.

Poro agents

By the 1920s, Poro had branches in 16 major cities in the United States and across the Caribbean. The company also had branches as far away as the Philippines.

Malone also expanded into the skin care business. In 1922, she launched a new face powder and skin care line promoting healthy and glowing skin.

In 1930, Malone moved again to a bigger city with one of the largest Black communities in the country—Chicago. The city had more than 200,000 Black residents. This was the perfect location to reach new customers.

Malone bought a whole city block and called it "Poro Block." It became the international headquarters for her company.

Unfortunately, Malone's business quickly declined in the 1930s. A costly divorce, lawsuits, and the Great Depression hurt her business. But Poro products continued to sell until the 1950s.

Malone at her home in Chicago around 1930

CHAPTER 4

THE GENEROUS BUSINESSWOMAN

Malone's success was not only in business but also in serving the community. She was a **philanthropist**. She used her wealth to make a difference in the lives of many people.

Malone helped support Black students' education. She donated money to Historically Black Colleges and Universities. She gave $25,000 to Howard University. She also supported students by providing scholarships for their education.

Malone also invested in the St. Louis community. She donated to the St. Louis YMCA, and she funded the St. Louis Colored Orphans' Home—now the Annie Malone Children & Family Service Center.

Wherever Malone saw a need, she made a difference. Communities still benefit from her efforts today.

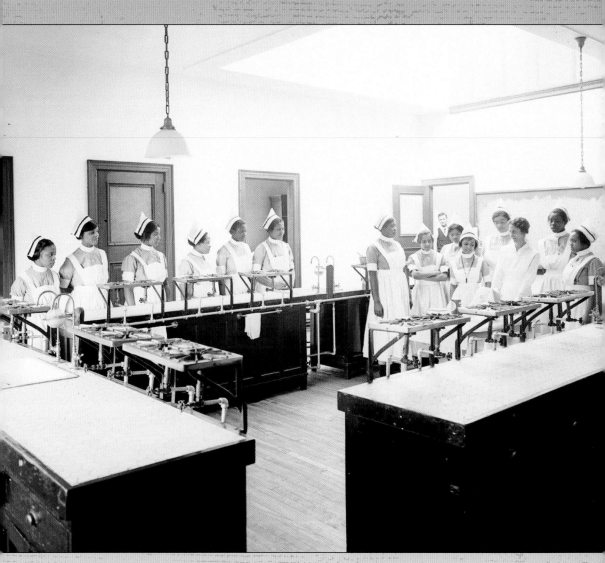

A nursing class at Howard University around 1915

FACT The May Day Parade in St. Louis has been renamed in Malone's honor. Now it is called the Annie Malone May Day Parade in recognition of her lasting impact on the St. Louis community.

CHAPTER 5

MALONE'S LEGACY

Malone inspired future generations of women in the hair care industry. She paved the way for Black women like Lisa Price, the founder of Carol's Daughter Hair Products. Like Malone, Price started small—in her kitchen. And like Malone, she sold products to women directly—one bottle at a time. Price sold her successful company to L'Oréal in 2014.

Shelley Davis created Kinky-Curly in 2003 to offer healthy products for women with curly, natural hair. She also used natural ingredients to create her hair care products.

Ayo Ogun created the Soultanicals Company in 2012. She created toxin-free, vegan hair products for women and girls with many different hair textures.

Malone's creativity and commitment made her a successful entrepreneur, an important support for her community, and a model for future Black businesswomen.

Lisa Price in 2014

FACT Black consumers continue to purchase products made specifically for their hair and support Black-owned businesses. Today, the Black hair care industry is worth $2.51 billion.

GLOSSARY

agent (AY-juhnt)—someone who acts on behalf of a business or person

consultant (kuhn-SUHL-tuhnt)—a person who teaches or gives advice to others

domestic (duh-MES-tik)—someone who works in another person's home

economy (ee-CON-uh-mee)—the ways in which a community handles its money and resources

Eurocentric (YOOR-oh-sen-trik)—focusing on European culture over other cultures

hygiene (HYE-jeen)—how well people keep themselves or their surroundings clean, especially to prevent disease

inquisitive (in-KWIZ-ih-tiv)—very curious; wanting more information

philanthropist (fih-LAN-thruh-pist)—a person who gives time or money to help others

regimen (REJ-uh-men)—a specific way of doing something

sanitation (san-uh-TAY-shuhn)—protecting people from dirt and disease, including by removing sewage and trash

sharecropper (SHAYR-crop-er)—one who works as a farmer on someone's land and gives a portion of the crops to the landowner

READ MORE

Lee, Sally. *Madam C.J. Walker: The Woman Behind Hair Care Products for African Americans.* North Mankato, MN: Capstone, 2020.

The Staff of The Undefeated. *The Fierce 44: Black Americans Who Shook Up the World.* Boston: Houghton Mifflin Harcourt, 2020.

Wilson, Jamia. *Young, Gifted and Black: Meet 52 Black Heroes from Past and Present.* Beverly, MA: Wide Eyed Editions / Quarto Group, 2018.

INTERNET SITES

Historic Missourians: Annie Turnbo Malone
historicmissourians.shsmo.org/annie-turnbo-malone

PBS: Our Remarkable Local History: Annie Turnbo Malone
pbs.org/video/annie-turnbo-malone-mei86d/

Smithsonian Institution: Annie Malone and Madam C.J. Walker
nmaahc.si.edu/explore/stories/annie-malone-and-madam-cj-walker-pioneers-african-american-beauty-industry

INDEX

ABOUT THE AUTHOR

Dr. Artika R. Tyner is a passionate educator, an award-winning author, a civil rights attorney, a sought-after speaker, and an advocate for justice. She lives in Saint Paul, Minnesota, and is the founder of the Planting People Growing Justice Leadership Institute.

— THE UNTOLD STORY OF —
ANNIE TURNBO MALONE

Most people know about Madam C.J. Walker's success
selling hair care products for Black women in the early
1900s. Before she started her own business, though,
she worked for Annie Turnbo Malone. Malone built a
huge business creating hair care and cosmetic products
for Black women. Uncover Malone's story and how it
connects to Walker's story.

FIRST BUT FORGOTTEN

Open a history book, and you'll probably see some familiar
names, such as Cesar Chavez and Rosa Parks. We learn a lot
about some historical figures, but not others. In this series, you'll
learn about some people you don't know—and how their stories
connect to the people you do know.

BOOKS IN THIS SERIES

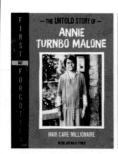

U. S. $7.99 | CAN $9.99

ISBN 978-1-66900-491-2

50799

9 781669 004912

capstone
capstonepub.com

F&P Text Level Gradient™
Officially Leveled by **Fountas & Pinnell**